COVERED BRIDGES

OF LANCASTER COUNTY ★ PENNSYLVANIA

Kenneth W. Collins

Designed and typeset by Lee Fitler

ISBN 0-9715932-0-5

𝔄 𝔖𝔱𝔢𝔯𝔩𝔦𝔫𝔤 𝔅𝔬𝔬𝔨
Printed by CPC/Science Press, Ephrata, PA

cover photo

Red Bank Bridge
This bridge, variously called Red Run or Red Run Grist Mill or Red Bank Bridge, was originally owned by
John Oberholtzer. As traffic increased in the area, Muddy Creek was rerouted to by-pass the bridge so
that a new concrete bridge could be built in 1926. The bridge is privately owned and not open for traffic.
However, the nearby campground has used it for church services in inclement weather.

To Nathanael and Benjamin,

my two sons, both of whom have undergone heart transplants. Their lives continue to be a source of strength and encouragement to all who know them. I love them dearly.

Acknowledgments

Thank you to Robert Navitski, Lancaster County Engineer, for his help in retrieving historical information from the bridge docket books in the county engineer's office. Thank you to Thomas Kipphorn, member of the Theodore Burr Covered Bridge Society of Pennsylvania, Lancaster, Pennsylvania, for his monumental work on the historical information provided in the appendix of this book. Thank you to the Lancaster County Historical Museum for guiding me in the collection of other historical information contained in this book. Thank you to my loving wife, Judy, who offered very helpful suggestions throughout the entire process of photographing, editing, designing and proofreading this publication.

TABLE OF CONTENTS

CONTENTS

This is a book of photographs. It is designed for those who want to see the covered bridges of Lancaster County, but do not have the time to visit them or prefer not to roam the beautiful roads of Lancaster County's idyllic countryside. For those who want to wander the rural roads, directions to each covered bridge are included. History buffs may find the book lacking in historical information. To you I can only say, there are some outstanding books that chronicle accounts of historical significance. Let me suggest Elizabeth Gipe Caruthers book, *Seeing Lancaster County's Covered Bridges: with exact locations,* or her article entitled, *"Elias McMellen, Forgotten Man,"* in the 1981 volume of Historical Papers and Addresses of Lancaster County Historical Society.

In 1923, D.F. Magee, Esq., published a detailed description of the waterways in Lancaster County, including the importance of bridges to the economy of the county, in an article entitled, *"The Old Wooden Covered Bridges of the Octoraro."* Another article of superb schol-arship, historical data and interesting anecdotes was written by Sister Mary Hildegarde Yeager, C.S.C., as part of her Master's thesis, entitled, *"Historic Bridge-Building in Lancaster*

County," published in 1937 (see bibliography for additional books). I felt no compulsion to reiterate what is available in other sources. My goal was to produce a book that would grace coffee tables in Lancaster County and offer tourists an opportunity to see part of our heritage not otherwise readily accessible to those with time constraints. Being a person who likes to travel, I have learned to appreciate how helpful pictures and books of local significance can be to those of us who are unable to visit all the points of interest of the localities to which we travel.

The photographs show the bridges in different seasons of the year, a labor of love that took four years and more film that I could have possibly imagined. With nearly 1000 photographs in my files, I felt that only a handful could be published without embarrassment. Over the years professionals and amateurs have taken many photographs of Lancaster County's covered bridges. If I could have selected from such a limitless supply, I am confident that this would have been an outstanding pictorial essay. I am satisfied with the results, however, and I hope you are too. Enjoy!

Willow Hill Bridge

Willow Hill Bridge was built from material salvaged from John Good's and Irwin Miller's farm bridges in 1962. The bridge is open to tourist traffic only.

Willow Hill Bridge

The interior of this bridge shows the Burr Arch Truss system of bridge building – developed by Theodore Burr in the late 1700's. Most existing covered bridges in Lancaster County were built using this truss system.

Baumgardner's Mill Bridge

Built in 1860, Baumgardner's Mill Bridge receives fewer visitors than most bridges because of its location, but its picturesque setting is worth the drive.

Hunsecker's Mill Bridge

Hunsecker's Mill Bridge, the longest single span covered bridge in the county, was originally built in 1848 by Joseph Russell. When Hurricane Agnes unleased her fury in 1972 the bridge was completely destroyed. After considerable dialogue with state and township officials, local citizens successfully saw the rebuilt bridge open in 1974 at a cost of $321,000.

Siegrist's Mill Bridge

Originally built in 1885 and known as Moore's Mill Bridge, this 70-foot structure has been called Siegrist's Mill Bridge since the Siegrist family bought the mill in 1895.

Keller's Mill Bridge

Elias McMellen built the original Keller's Mill Bridge in 1873. He rebuilt it 18 years later following extensive flood damage. It is the only white covered bridge left in the county. This bridge is also referred to as Rettew's Mill and Guy Bard's Mill Bridge. The original four-story mill building burned down and was replaced by a two-story building, the remains of which are next to the bridge.

Colemanville Bridge

Washed away in 1938 and again in 1992, the Colemanville Bridge, at 170 feet, is the county's second longest single-span bridge still in use. If you visit the bridge, look closely on the south side of the bridge and you will see the old trolley car right-of-way heading east along the creek.

Risser's Mill Bridge

Risser's Mill Bridge spans Little Chiques. The mill was originally owned by Peter Horst and was built in 1816 according to the date above the entrance door on the inside.

Pine Grove Bridge

Pine Grove Bridge was originally built 16 years after the first covered bridge was built in Philadelphia in 1800. It has been rebuilt twice, once in 1846 and again in 1884. At 204 feet in length, it is the only remaining double-span, double-arch bridge in the county and is jointly owned by Lancaster and Chester counties.

Jackson's Sawmill Bridge

Built in 1878 for $2,410, Jackson's Sawmill Bridge is one of only two bridges known to be built by Samuel Stauffer. After the flood of 1985 destroyed the bridge, it was rebuilt 3 feet higher to avoid future flood damage.

Zook's Mill Bridge

Zook's Mill Bridge rebuffed the fury of Hurricane Agnes in 1972. Inside the bridge is a sign that marks the water level 6.5 feet above the bridge floor. A total of 17.5 feet of water inundated the creek with its nooks, valleys and surrounding farm land. This bridge is also known as Wenger's Mill Bridge.

Shearer's Mill Bridge

Originally built in 1847, Jacob Shearer's Mill Covered Bridge cost $600. Nine years later, a flood destroyed it and it was rebuilt by Jacob Clare. Scheduled to be replaced by a concrete bridge in 1970, local citizens successfully negotiated its removal to Memorial Park next to the high school in Manheim. It is open to pedestrians only.

Weaver's Mill Bridge

Just north of Churchtown on Weaverland Road, you will find Weaver's Mill Bridge. The mill was built in 1878 and originally owned by Isaac Shearer. The old sawmill building, now a chicken house, is next to the nearby farm house.

Bitzer's Mill Bridge

Built in 1846, Bitzer's Mill Bridge is the oldest covered bridge still in use in Lancaster County, although it has been substantially rebuilt using steel "I" beams under the wooden floor, which accounts for the unusually high weight limit of 20 tons. All other covered wooden bridges are restricted to 5 tons or less. Bitzer's Mill Bridge is known by several different names: Martin's Mill, Eberly's Cider Mill, and Fiantz's Mill, all earlier mill owners.

Pool Forge Bridge

Although Pool Forge Bridge remains, it is privately owned and closed to traffic. History records that President James Buchanan met his fiance at Pool Forge but she died before they could be married and he remained a bachelor.

Pine Forge Bridge
is incorrect. This
is the Pool Forge
Covered Bridge.

Pine Forge Bridge

On the center Burr truss you will find "ELIAS McMELLEN A.D. 1859" engraved in the wood. While Levi Fink appears as the builder of record, the carving suggests that, at the very least, Elias McMellen worked on this bridge. The base of Pine Forge Bridge shows how the Burr Trusses rest on concrete abutments supporting the entire bridge.

Neff's Mill Bridge

One of the narrowest covered bridges is Neff's Mill Bridge with a width of 11 feet. In the winter of 2001, the mill was torn down and the stones used to make a fence on the property.

Kurtz Mill Bridge

Kurtz Mill Bridge was originally known as Isaac Bean's Mill Bridge when it was built in 1876 by W.W. Upp for $1407. When Hurricane Agnes destroyed the bridge in 1972, it was relocated and rebuilt in Lancaster County Central Park south of Lancaster City.

Mercer's Mill Bridge

Located just south of Christiana, Mercer's Mill Bridge is one of only two remaining bridges shared with Chester County. It was built by B.J. Carter in 1880.

Erb's Mill Bridge

Originally built in 1849 for $700, Erb's Mill Bridge opened for traffic
just as the "Gold Rush" beckoned 80,000+ people to California.

Eshleman's Mill Bridge

Sometimes referred to as Paradise Bridge, Eshleman's Mill Bridge was built by Elias McMellen in 1865, the year Abraham Lincoln was assassinated.

White Rock Forge Bridge

White Rock or White Rock Forge Bridge was built in 1847 by John Russell. It has been washed away and rebuilt twice. It is Lancaster County's second oldest covered bridge still in use.

Landis' Mill Bridge

At 53 feet in length, the shortest covered bridge still in use by vehicles is Landis' Mill Bridge, located 1 block west of Park City Mall on Station Road. Unlike his other bridges, Elias McMellen built this bridge in 1873 using the Kingpost truss rather than the usual Burr Arch truss.

Forry's Mill Bridge

Elias McMellen built Forry's Mill Bridge in 1869, the year
the first transcontinental railroad was completed.

Lime Valley Bridge

The only bridge known to be built by Joseph Cramer is Lime Valley Bridge built in 1871. It was originally known as Huntzinger's Mill Bridge. Cramer's short building career may have been due, in part, to the $3500 cost, which was 10% higher than the other established builders. If Elias McMellen had not been building Harnish's Sawmill Bridge, he may have been contracted to build this bridge.

Shenck's Mill Bridge

Built in 1847, Shenck's Mill Bridge is the only Charles Melhorn bridge still in use. It is the third oldest bridge still open to traffic. However, the present bridge was partially rebuilt by Levi Fink in 1855. Shenck is also spelled Shenk or Schenck.

Pinetown Bridge

There is an interesting story about the rebuilding of the Pinetown Bridge in Elizabeth Gipe Caruthers' book *Seeing Lancaster County's Covered Bridges*. After it was washed off its concrete base during Hurricane Agnes, it floated down the Conestoga River just missing Hunsecker's Mill Bridge about a mile downstream. Amish worker's in the area disassembled the damaged bridge, carried the pieces back upstream, and reassembled the bridge. At its raised height of 17.5 feet, it is higher off the water surface than any other covered wooden bridge in the county.

Kaufman's Distillery Mill Bridge

Kauffman's Distillery Mill was one of over 130 distilleries in the county in the late 1800s. Built in 1857, the bridge is one of nine covered bridges built by James Carpenter.

Herr's Mill Bridge

Another bridge no longer opened to traffic is the Herr's Mill Bridge, originally built in 1844. Located just south of Hwy 30 on Ronks Road, this double-span bridge is 178 feet in length and is also known as the Souderburg Bridge.

Bucher's Mill Bridge

Built by Elias McMellen in 1881, Bucher's Mill Bridge was destroyed and rebuilt the following year. At 68 feet in length, it is the second shortest covered bridge still in use.

Brubaker's Bridge

Harold Brubaker's Bridge is located in a roadside park one mile southeast of Strasburg.

Eichelberger's Mill Bridge

Eichelberger's Mill Bridge was moved to Buck Hill Farm in 1966

APPENDIX

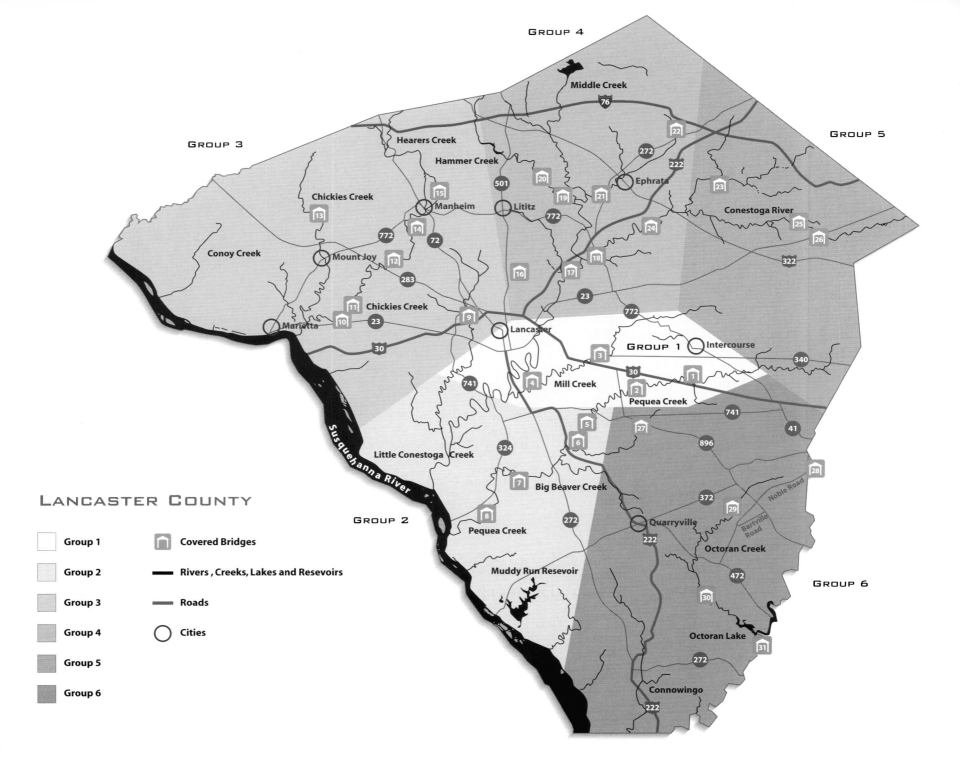

LANCASTER COUNTY

Group 1
Group 2
Group 3
Group 4
Group 5
Group 6

Covered Bridges

Rivers , Creeks, Lakes and Resevoirs

Roads

Cities

Ask the average person browsing the quaint shops in any of Lancaster County's tourist areas where the covered bridges are located and you may get directions to one or two, if you are lucky, because the person is likely to be one of our welcomed visitors as well. Even talking to one of the locals you may fair no better since many Lancastrians have not visited all the covered bridges themselves. If they have, it is still unlikely you will be given reliable directions to the more remote locations.

For those who would like to visit the bridges, I have provided simple directions from the nearest major intersection to each bridge. In some cases, however, a road map may still be helpful. It is very unlikely that you will be able to see all the covered bridges in one day and still appreciate their scenic beauty, not to mention snapping a picture or two of each bridge. Of course, if your goal is just to take a quick peek and move on, you can make it, but hold onto your hat!

To make your adventure easier and more enjoyable, I have divided the bridges into six groups. Others may suggest their favorite route, and that's okay. Use whatever works for you.

1. Eshleman's Mill Covered Bridge (also called Paradise Covered Bridge):
from the intersection of Hwy. 30 and Belmont Road (at the east end of Paradise), take Belmont Road north 1/2 mile to bridge

2. Herr's Mill Covered Bridge (privately owned, not open to traffic):
from Eshleman's Mill Covered Bridge, retrace your path to Hwy. 30, go west on Hwy. 30 to Ronks Road (1 1/2 miles west of Paradise), take Ronks Road south 1/2 mile

3. Willow Hill Covered Bridge (open to tourist traffic only):
from Herr's Mill Covered Bridge, retrace your path to Hwy 30, go west on Hwy. 30 approximately 1 mile to bridge on right (across from Rockvale Shopping Mall)

4. Kurtz's Mill Covered Bridge (located in Lancaster County Central Park):
from the Willow Hill Covered Bridge, continue on Hwy. 30 west to Strasburg Pike (approx. 2 1/4 miles), turn left on Strasburg Pike to Millport Road (1/4 mile), turn right on Millport Road to Eshleman Mill Road (approx. 2 miles), turn left on Eshleman Mill Road to Golf Road (approx. 1/2 mile), turn right on Golf Road and follow the sign to the bridge

5. Neff's Mill Covered Bridge:

from Kurtz's Mill Covered Bridge, reverse your directions to Millport Road, turn right on Millport Road to Lampeter Road, turn right on Lampeter Road to Penn Grant Road (approx. 3 1/2 miles), turn left on Penn Grant Road to bridge (approx. 1/2 mile)

6. Lime Valley Covered Bridge:

from Neff's Mill Covered Bridge, go back west on Penn Grant Road to Pequea Lane (approx. 1/4 mile), turn left on Pequea Lane to Lime Valley Road (approx. 1 mile), turn right on Lime Valley Road to bridge (approx. 1/2 mile)

7. Baumgardner's Mill Covered Bridge:

from Lime Valley Covered Bridge, continue south on Breneman Road to Church Street in the village of Refton (you will cross Hwy. 222 and go to 2 blocks to Church St., turn right on Church Street to Refton Road (1/4 mile), turn left on Refton Road to Smithville Road (1/4 mile), turn right on Smithville Road to Byerland Church Road (3/4 mile -- Smithville Road turns south and Byerland Church Road continues straight ahead), stay on Byerland Church Road (you will cross Hwy. 272, 1/2 mile after you get on Byerland Church Road), continue on Byerland Church Road to Byerland Mennonite Church (approx. 1 3/4 miles), continue straight ahead and the road becomes Covered Bridge Road, stay on Covered Bridge Road to bridge (approx. 3/4 mile).

8. Colemanville Covered Bridge (you will now see one of the more remote bridges):

from Baumgardner's Mill Bridge, continue south on Covered Bridge Road to Frogtown Road (approx. 1/2 mile), turn right on Frogtown Road to Hwy. 324, aka Marticville Road (approx. 1/2 mile), turn left on Hwy. 324 to Fox Hollow Road (approx. 3 miles, the road becomes narrow and very winding at times, but stay on course), turn left on Fox Hollow Road -- it looks almost like someone's driveway and is easily missed -- to bridge (approx. 1/4 mile).

9. Landis' Mill Covered Bridge:
from the intersection of Hwy. 30 and Harrisburg Pike near the Park City Mall, take Harrisburg Pike to Plaza Blvd. on the west side of the mall, turn right on Plaza Blvd to Station Road (approx. 1/4 mile), turn left on Station Road to bridge (1 block).

10. Forry's Mill Covered Bridge:
from Landis' Mill Covered Bridge, retrace your path back to Harrisburg Pike, turn right on Harrisburg Pike to Hwy 741 (approx. 3/4 mile), turn left on Hwy. 741 to Marietta Pike (approx. 1 mile, you will cross over Hwy. 30), turn right on Marietta Pike to Bridge Valley Road (approx. 6 miles), turn right on Bridge Valley Road to bridge (approx. 1/4 mile); warning: Bridge Valley Road makes a sharp left after 1 block.

11. Siegrist's Mill Covered Bridge:
from Forry's Mill Covered Bridge, retrace your path back to Marietta Pike, turn left on Marietta Pike to Prospect Road (approx. 1 mile), turn left on Prospect Road to Siegrist Road (approx. 1/2 mile), turn left on Siegrist Road to bridge (approx. 1/2 mile).

12. Shenck's Mill Covered Bridge:
from Siegrist's Mill Covered Bridge, retrace your path back to Prospect Road, turn left on Prospect Road over Hwy. 283 (at this point Prospect Road becomes Spooky Nook Road) to Shenck Road (approx 1/2 mile past Hwy. 283), turn left on Shenck Road to bridge (approx. 3/4 mile)

13. Risser's Mill Covered Bridge (old mill building is next to the bridge):
from Shenck's Mill Covered Bridge, the easiest route, though not the most direct, is to retrace your path back to Hwy. 283, get on Hwy. 283 west to Hwy. 772 (approx. 2 1/2 miles), turn left on Hwy. 772 to Milton Grove Road (approx. 1 1/2 miles), turn right on Milton Grove Road to Mt. Pleasant Road (approx. 1 1/2 miles), turn left on Mt. Pleasant Road to bridge (approx. 1/2 mile)

14. Kauffman's Distillery Covered Bridge:
from Risser's Mill Covered Bridge, retrace your path back to Hwy. 772 (there are other back roads you can take, but you are very likely to get lost), turn left on Hwy. 772 to Sun Hill Road (approx. 5 miles), turn right on Sun Hill Road to bridge (approx. 1/4 mile)

15. Shearer's Mill Covered Bridge (open to pedestrians only):
from Kauffman's Distillery Covered Bridge, retrace your path back to Hwy. 772, turn right on Hwy.772 to Laurel Street (approx. 1/4 mile after you cross Hwy. 72 in Manheim) turn left on Laurel Street to Adele Avenue (2 long blocks), turn right on Adele Avenue to bridge (approx. 3 blocks)

16. Eichelberger's Mill Covered Bridge (privately owned, not open to traffic)
from the intersection of Hwy. 501 and Millport Road (at the northwest corner of the Lancaster Airport), take Hwy 501 (Lititz Pike) north 1/4 mile to Buck Hill Farm (private driveway on right); request permission from owners to see bridge

17. Hunsecker's Mill Covered Bridge:
from the intersection of Hwy. 30 and Hwy. 23 (New Holland Pike), take Hwy. 23 east to Mondale Road (approx. 2 1/4 miles), turn left on Mondale to Hunsecker Road (approx. 1/4 mile), turn left on Hunsecker Road to bridge (approx. 1/4 mile)

18. Pinetown Covered Bridge:
from Hunsecker's Mill Covered Bridge, retrace your path to Mondale Road, turn left on Mondale Road to Bridge Road (approx. 1 mile), turn left on Bridge Road to bridge (approx. 1/2 mile)

19. Zook's Mill Covered Bridge:
from Pinetown Covered Bridge, continue west over bridge 50 feet to Pinetown Road, turn right to Bushong Road (approx. 1/2 mile), turn left on Bushong Road to Hwy. 272 (aka Oregon Pike -- 1/2 mile), turn right on Hwy. 272 to Rose Hill Road (approx. 3/4 mile), turn left on Rose Hill Road to bridge (1/2 mile)

20. Erb's Mill Covered Bridge:
from Zook's Mill Covered Bridge, retrace your path to Hwy. 272, turn left on Hwy. 272 to Newport Road (approx. 1 mile), turn left on Newport Road to Picnic Woods Road in Rothville (approx. 2 1/2 miles -- watch carefully for this road), turn right on Picnic Woods Road to bridge (approx. 1 1/4 miles)

21. Keller's Mill Covered Bridge:
from Erb's Mill Covered Bridge, retrace your path to Newport Road, turn left on Newport Road to Rothville Road (approx. 1/2 mile), turn left on Rothville Road to Rettew Mill Road (approx. 2 1/2 miles), turn left on Rettew Mill Road to bridge (approx. 1/4 mile)

22. Bucher's Mill Covered Bridge:
from Keller's Mill Covered Bridge, retrace your path back to Rothville Road, turn left on Rothville Road to Hwy. 272 (approx. 1/4 mile), turn left on Hwy. 272 and follow it through Ephrata towards Reamstown until you come to Creek Road, just 50 feet after you cross over Cocalico Creek (approx. 2 1/4 miles), turn right on Creek Road to bridge (approx. 1/4 mile)

23. Red Run Covered Bridge (privately owned, not open to traffic):
from Bucher's Mill Covered Bridge, retrace your path back to Hwy. 272, turn right on Hwy. 272 to Church Road (approx. 1/2 mile), turn right on Church Road to Red Run Road (approx. 1 3/4 miles -- look carefully, don't miss Red Run Road), turn left on Red Run Road to bridge (approx. 1 3/4 miles)

24. Bitzer's Mill Covered Bridge:
from Red Run Covered Bridge, continue south on Gristmill Road to Hwy. 322 (approx. 2 3/4 miles), turn right on Hwy. 322 to Cabin Road (approx. 2 1/4 miles), turn left on Cabin Road to Cider Mill Road (approx. 1 1/4 miles), turn left on Cider Mill Road to bridge (1/4 mile)

25. Weaver's Mill Covered Bridge:
from Bitzer's Mill Covered Bridge, retrace your path back to Hwy. 322, turn right on Hwy. 322 to Weaverland Road (approx. 2 1/2 miles), turn left on Weaverland Road to Hwy. 897 (approx. 1 mile), turn right on Hwy. 897 for 1/4 mile, turn left back onto Weaverland Road, continue on Weaverleand Road to bridge (approx. 2 3/4 miles -- at about the 2 1/2 mile point, Weaverland Road curves left and Brendle Road goes straight ahead)

26. Pool Forge Covered Bridge (privately owned, not open to traffic):
from Weaver's Mill Bridge, continue on Weaverland Road to Churchtown Road (approx. 1/2 mile), turn right on Churchtown Road to Pool Forge Road (approx. 1 mile), turn right on Pool Forge Road to Hwy. 23 (approx. 1/2 mile), turn right on Hwy. 23 for about 150 feet and turn left on Pool Forge Road again to bridge (approx. 1/4 mile); if you politely ask the owners who live in the nearby historic stone house, you may receive permission to see the bridge up close

27. Brubaker's Farm Covered Bridge (privately owned):
from the east end of Strasburg where Hwy. 896 and Hwy. 741 split, take Hwy. 896 (Georgetown Road) south to Reservoir Road (approx. 1 mile), turn right on Reservoir Road to park entrance on left (approx. 1/4 mile)

28. Mercer's Mill Covered Bridge (owned jointly by Lancaster and Chester Counties):
from the intersection of Hwy. 30 and Hwy. 41 in Gap, take Hwy. 41 south to Hwy. 372 (approx. 2 1/4 miles), turn right on Hwy. 372 to Newport Turnpike in Atglen (1/4 mile), turn left on Newport Turnpike to Steelville Road (approx. 1/4 mile), turn right on Steelville Road to Creek Road (approx. 3/4 mile), turn left on Creek Road to Bailey Crossroads Road (approx. 1/2 mile), turn left on Bailey Crossroads Road to bridge (1/4 mile)

29. Jackson's Sawmill Covered Bridge (now you will see the least visited bridge):
from Mercer's Mill Covered Bridge, retrace your path back to Steelville Road, turn left on Steelville Road to Noble Road (approx. 1/4 mile), turn left on Noble to Mt. Pleasant Road (approx. 5 1/4 miles -- you will cross Hwy. 896), turn right on Mt. Pleasant Road to bridge (approx. 1 mile)

30. White Rock Forge Covered Bridge (far from the "maddening crowd"):
from Jackson's Sawmill Covered Bridge, retrace your path back to Noble Road, turn right on Noble Road to White Rock Forge Road (approx. 4 1/4 miles -- you will cross Hwy. 472), turn left on White Rock Forge Road to bridge (approx. 1 1/4 miles)

31. Pine Grove Covered Bridge (double-span bridge; owned jointly by Lancaster and Chester Counties):
from White Rock Forge Covered Bridge, proceed across bridge to King Pen Road, turn left on King Pen Road to Ashville Road -- watch road signs very carefully (approx. 1 1/4 miles), turn left on Ashville Road to bridge (approx. 3 miles); to get back to "civilization", continue over bridge to Street Road (1/4 mile), turn left on Street Road to Hwy. 472 (approx. 1 1/2 miles); left on Hwy. 472 takes you to Quarryville (Lancaster County), right on Hwy. 472 takes you to Oxford (Chester County)

Bridges built by Elias McMellen

1859 Yohn's Mill/Pool Forge Bridge
1865 Eshleman's Mill Bridge
1866 Ressler's Mill Bridge
1866 Red Run Bridge (Joseph Oberholtzer's Mill Bridge 1)
1867 Miller & Nolt's Point Mill Bridge
1867 Printer's Paper Mill Bridge
1868 Wabash Mill Bridge
1868 Stoneroad's Mill Bridge
1868 Pequea Valley Tavern Bridge
1869 Forry's Mill Bridge
1870 New Milltown Bridge
1871 Miller's Mill Bridge
1871 Lime Valley Mill Twin #2 Bridge
1871 Harnish's Sawmill Bridge
1872 Risser's Mill Bridge
1872 Gable's Fording Bridge
1873 Landis' Mill Bridge
1873 Keller's Mill Bridge
1874 Spring Grove Mill Bridge
1874 Oberholtzer's Mill Bridge
1874 Emanuel Cassel's Mill Bridge
1875 Amwake's Mill Bridge
1881 Bucher's Mill Bridge
1884 Pine Grove Bridge
1884 Dorsey's Mill Bridge
1886 Nolt's Mill Bridge
1892 Good's Mill Bridge
1892 Aberdeen Mill Bridge
1893 London Vale/Leaman's Mill Bridge

Bridges rebuilt or repaired by Elias McMellen

1867 Johnson's Mill Bridge
1867 Lutz's Boring Mill Bridge
1867 Old Factory Mill Bridge
1868 Clonmell Bridge
1870 6th Lock/Zercher's Mill Bridge
1874 Kauffman's Mill Bridge
1875 Musselman's Mill Bridge
1881 Sensenig's Mill Bridge
1884 King's Bridge
1884 Martic Forge Bridge
1884 White Rock Forge Bridge
1891 Keller's Mill Bridge
1891 Lutz's Boring Mill Bridge again
1892 Bucher's Mill Bridge
1893 Eshleman's Mill Bridge
1902 Harnish's Sawmill Bridge

Elias McMellen may have built and rebuilt or repaired other bridges, but there is no official mention of his name in the Bridge Docket or county records that I could find connecting him to such bridges

Those who built at least 4 bridges

James Carpenter

1846 Lintner's Mill Bridge

1851 Pusey's Mill Bridge

1852 David Landis' Mill Bridge

1856 Colemanville Bridge

1856 New Milltown Bridge (same place Elias McMellen built a new bridge 1870)

1857 Kauffman's Mill Bridge (the same bridge rebuilt by Elias McMellen in 1874)

1866 No name given: over Conestoga River at Safe Harbor on River Road (the same bridge rebuilt by Elias McMellen in 1870 blown away by high winds)

1884 Blackrock Forge Bridge

1885 Siegrist Mill Bridge

Robert Russell

1843 Bushong's Mill Bridge (with Joseph Elliot)

1844 Daniel Pott's Mill Bridge (with Joseph Elliot)

1845 John Weaver's Mill Bridge (wtih Joseph Elliot)

1848 King's Bridge (same place Elias McMellen built new bridge in 1884)

1850 Bellbank Bridge

1861 Bellbank Bridge rebuilt

George Fink

1841 Kafroth's Mill Bridge

1846 Bitzer's Mill Bridge

1846 Martin's Mill Bridge (with Samuel Reamsnyder) (this may be the same bridge called Bitzer's Mill Bridge; records inconclusive)

1847 Steelville Mill (with George Cinkle)

Charles Malhorn

1845 Mt. Joy Waterworks Bridge

1846 Aaron Martin's Mill Bridge

1846 Kerr's Sawmill Bridge

1847 Shenk's Mill Bridge

Levi Fink

1855 Keener's Mill Bridge

1855 Nylin's Mill Bridge

1859 Pool Forge Bridge (Elias McMellen's name is carved on the center truss inside the bridge)

1859 Sickman's Mill Bridge

Silas Wolverton

1857 Col. George Mayer's Bridge

1858 Nylin's Mill Bridge (not same bridge noted above)

1859 Neff's Mill Bridge

1859 Sensenig's Mill Bridge

World Bridge #	Name(s) of Bridge	Builder(s)	Year Built or Rebuilt	Cost	Truss Type	Spans	Overall Length	Abutment to Abutment
Big Beaver Creek								
38-36-56F.	Mylin's / Beck's Mill	Silas Wolverton	1858	$800	Burr	1	69ft	60ft
36-57	John Strohm's Mill	John Strohm	1837	$1,200	Burr	1	89ft	81ft
36-27	Samuel Miller's Mill	Elias McMellen	1856	n/a	Burr	1	75ft	63ft
Little Beaver Creek								
36-48	Harold Brubaker's Farm	Harold Brubaker	1969	$550	Stringer	1	28ft 1in	19ft 6in
36-58	Daniel Herr's	Joseph Russell	1855	$1,397	Burr	1	80ft	64ft
Big Chiques Creek								
36-31	Jacob Shearer's Cider Mill	Jacob Clare	1856	$1,197	Burr	1	88ft 6in	73ft
36-32	Kauffman's Distillery	James C. Carpenter	1857	n/a	Burr	1	96f	83ft 5in
36-30	Henry Shenck's Mil	Charles Melhorn	1847	$650	Burr	1	96ft 3in	80ft
36-133	Joseph Bender's Mill	Samuel Hopkins	1850	$1,194	Burr	1	117f	105ft
36-59	John Hertzler Moore's Mill 1	John Weimer	1879	$1,667	Burr	1	95ft	85ft
36-60	John Hertzler Moore's Mill 2				Burr	1	70ft	57ft
36-37	Michael Moore's Mill	James C. Carpenter	1885	$1,872	Burr	1	101ft 6in	92ft
36-28	John Forry's Mill	Elias McMellen	1869	$2,969	Burr	1	103ft	90ft
36-29	Amwake's Mill	Elias McMellen	1875	$2,447	Burr	1	133ft	123ft
36-61	Musselman"s Mill	Israel Cooper	1838	$1,598	Burr	1	120ft	110ft
36-134	Chiques Furnace				Burr	1	120ft	
Little Chiques Creek								
36-62	Joseph Keener's/Heistand's	Levi Fink / Nicholas Brown	1855	$918	Burr	1	68ft	56ft
36-63	Baker's Mill	Samuel Hopkins	1849	n/a	Burr	1	68ft	56ft
36-64	Mt. Joy Waterworks Mill	Charles Melhorn	1845	$900	Burr	1	95ft	83ft
36-65	Emanuel Cassel's	Elias McMellen	1874	$1,569	Burr	1	75ft	63ft
36-35	Johnson's/Musselman's	William Dietrich	1854	$950	Burr	1	80ft	70ft
36-36	Risser's Mill	Elias McMellen	1872	$1,525	Burr	1	82ft	69ft 7in
Cocalico Creek								
36-12	Monroe Bucher's Mill	Elias McMellen	1881	$1,167	Burr	1	73ft 3in	63ft 10in
36-67	Wabash Mill	Elias McMellen	1868	n/a	Burr	1	102ft	93ft
36-68	John Graver's Mil	Samuel Reamsnyder	1848	$835	Burr	1	76ft	66ft
36-13	Henry Keller's Mil	Elias McMellen	1873	$2,075	Burr	1	73ft 9in	63ft 3in
36-69	John Stoll's Mill	n/a	1840	n/a	Burr	1	99ft	94ft
36-70	Colonel George Mayer's	Silas Wolverton	1859	$898	Burr	1	79ft	69ft
36-14	John Wenger's Mill	Henry Zook	1849	$700	Burr	1	89ft	76ft
36-66	Jesse Lutz's Boring Mill	George Sweigart/Jesse Lutz	1852	$500	Burr	1	69ft	61ft
Conestoga River								
36-01	Pool Forge/Yohn's Mill	Levi Fink / Elias McMellen	1859	$1,219	Burr	1	99ft 5in	84ft 5in
36-02	Isaac Shearer's / Weaver's	B.J.Carter / J.W. Stauffer	1878	$1,468	Burr	1	88ft	79ft
36-71	Spring Grove Mill	Elias McMellen	1874	$3,747	Burr	1	133ft	120ft
36-72	Conestoga Roller Mill	E.C. Deets	1881	$1,851	Burr	1	112ft	104ft
36-73	Aaron Martin's Mill	Charles Malhorn	1846	$1,449	Burr	1	149ft	134ft
36-74	White Oak Mill / Nolt's Mill	Elias McMellen	1866	$2,700	Burr	1	103ft	91ft
36-75	Israel Sensenig's Mill	Silas Wolverton	1857	n/a	Burr	1	65ft	60ft

Roadway Width	Opening Height	Height from Water	Road Information	Comments	Extant
4ft	12ft 6in	8ft 3in	Main St. / LR 36015, SR 2019	Year gone: 1920	
13ft	12ft 6in	6ft	Refton Rd / SR 3021, T 498	Flooded: 8/7/1882	
13ft	12ft 9in	11ft 6in	Smithville Rd / LR 36091, SR 3040	Rebuilt by E. McMellen in 1871/$1,875; year gone: 5/1961	
12f	8ft 3in	3ft	Private road off Hwy 896	Rebuilt in 1973; still in existence, but privately owned	✓
14ft	13ft	16f	Breneman Rd / T 498	Flooded: 6/26/1938	
14ft 5in	12ft 7in	6ft	S. Colebrook Rd / T 374 - moved in 1971	Moved to Manheim Memorial Park at cost of $12,000	✓
13ft 7in	12ft 3in	9ft	Sun Hill Rd / T 889	Still in use	✓
14ft 6in	12ft 8in	10ft	Erisman Rd / T 372	Rebuilt in 1855 for $837; still in use	✓
14ft	13ft	11ft	Eby Chiques Rd / T 364	Flooded: late 1925	
14ft	12ft	8ft	Garfield Rd / T 359 & T 369	Year gone: 1922	
14ft	12ft	9ft	S. Garfield Rd / T 360 & T 367	Year gone: 1922	
13ft 10in	12ft 1in	10ft 6in	Siegrist Rd / T 360 & T 361	Still in use; now called Siegrist's Mill	✓
13ft 8in	12ft 5in	8ft	Bridge Valley Rd / T 362 & T 365	Still in use	✓
12ft 6in	12ft	13ft	old arm of Kinderhook Rd / LR 36067	Year gone: 1962	
15ft 6in	13ft 5in	16ft	Marietta Pike / SR 0023	Year gone: ca. 1941	
			Hwy. 44	Year gone: 1908 ?	
15ft	13ft 6in	9ft 6in	Cloverleaf Rd / T 334; Sunnyside Rd / T 855	Year gone: 1926	
14ft	12ft	9ft	Milton Grove Rd / LR 36067, SR 4033	Flooded: 7/22/1945	
14ft	12ft 6in	12ft	Manheim St /LR 36002; Mt. Joy Rd / SR 0772	Year gone: 1920	
14ft	12ft 6in	8ft	Longenecker Rd / LR 36067, SR 4003	Flooded: 10/1/1934	
12ft	12ft	7ft	Drager Rd / T356	Rebuilt By E. McMellen, 1867 / $1,650; Flooded: 6/22/1972	
11ft 9in	12ft 8in	9ft	Mt. Pleasant Rd / LR 36069, SR 4010	Still in use	✓
14ft 10in	12ft 6in	9ft	Cocalico Creek Rd / T 955	Rebuilt by E. McMellen in 1892/$1,025; still in use	✓
12ft	12ft	7ft	Wabash Rd / T 670	Flooded (?): 1936	
14ft	13ft	9ft	Old Mill Rd / LR 36060, SR 1045	Year gone: 1923	
13ft 7in	12ft 6in	9ft	Rettew Mill Rd / T 656	Rebuilt by E. McMellen in 1891/$1,250; still in use	✓
15ft	11ft	12ft	Rothville's Rd / LR 36060, SR 1011	Flooded (?): 1917	
14ft	13ft	10ft	Newport Rd / Hwy 772 - SR 0772	Year gone: 1921	
14ft	12ft 6in	8ft	Log Cabin Rd / T 797	Still in use	✓
14ft	12ft 6in	8ft	Ridge Rd / LR 36013, SR 1030	Rebuilt by E. McMellen in 1891 for $1,480; year gone: 1921	
14ft	13ft	8ft	Pool Forge Rd / LR 36053	Still in existence, but privately owned	✓
13ft 8in	2ft 6in	10ft	Weaverland Rd / T 773	Still in use	✓
16ft 7in	13ft	10ft	Spring Grove Rd / LR 36055, SR 1021	Year gone: 1927	
14ft	13ft	8ft	Reading Rd / SR 0625	Year gone: 1914	
13ft	13ft	10ft	Linden Rd / T 909; old part of Weaverland Rd	Year gone: 1922	
12ft 8in	12ft 6in	8ft	White Oak Rd / T 810	Flooded (?): 1936	
2ft	12ft	8ft	Gristmill Rd / T 783, T 600	Rebuilt by E. McMellen in 1881 for $1,034; year gone: 1957	

World Bridge #	Name(s) of Bridge	Builder(s)	Year Built or Rebuilt	Cost	Truss Type	Spans	Overall Length	Abutment to Abutment
36-76	George Hinkle's Mill	John Black	1838	$5,240	Burr	3	303ft	293ft
36-04	Bitzer's Mill	G. Fink / S. Reamsnyder	1846	$1.12	Burr	1	99ft 6in	86ft 6in
36-77	Joel or Clayton Wenger's	J. Elliot / R. Russell	1845	$1,100	Burr	1	142ft	130ft
36-78	Kafroth's / Greybill's Mill	J. Fink / S. Reamsnyder	1841	$1,299	Burr	1	140ft	128ft
36-79	Bushong's Mill	J. Elliot / R. Russell	1843	$2,389	Double Burr	1	195ft	180ft
36-05	Pinetown / Nolt's Point Mill	Elias McMellen	1867	$4,500	Burr	1	135ft	119ft 7in
36-06	Amos Hunsecker's Mill	Joseph Russell	1848	$1,988	Double Burr	1	180ft	169ft 6in
36-80	Printer's Paper Mill	Elias McMellen	1867	$1,650	Double Burr	2	306ft	295ft 8in
36-07	Eden / Umbel's Mill	Israel W. Groff	1848	$1,790	Double Burr	1	156ft	146ft
36-81	Hardwicke Railroad Bridge	W.R. Wilton / A. Campbell	1830	$30,000	Town Lattice	11	1,400ft	n/a
36-11	County Home	n/a	n/a	n/a	Boxed Pony	6	200ft	195ft
36-82	Old Factory / Humesville	Deller & Co.	1853	n/a	Burr	2	210ft 6in	205ft
36-83	Reigart's Landing	n/a	1845	n/a	Burr	1	165ft	156ft
36-84	Engleside Mill / Graeff's	Miller / Hoover	1824	n/a	Double Burr	2	317ft 6in	306ft
36-85	Engleside Railroad Bridge	n/a	1885	n/a	Howe	2	279ft	279ft
36-86	1st Lock / Light's or Levan's	n/a	n/a	n/a	Double Burr	2	263ft	251ft
36-08	2nd Lock / Snavely's Mill	Abraham Snavely	1836	n/a	Double Burr	2	349ft	339ft
36-09	3rd Lock / Wabank Mill	John Black	1835	$3,500	Burr	2	246ft	236ft
36-87	4th Lock / Slackwater Mill	J. Ohmit / J. Witmer	1839	$4,300	Double Burr	2	269ft	256ft
36-88	5th Lock / Rock Hill Tavern	Jacob G. Peters	1858	$3,592.75	Double Burr	2	273ft	257ft 6in
36-89	6th Lock / Zercher's Mill	John Black	1838	$4,900	Double Burr	2	295ft	282ft

Little Conestoga Creek

World Bridge #	Name(s) of Bridge	Builder(s)	Year Built or Rebuilt	Cost	Truss Type	Spans	Overall Length	Abutment to Abutment
36-16	Jacob Landis' Mill	Elias McMellen	1873	$969	Kingpost	1	53ft	40ft
36-136	Rohrerstown Railroad Br	James Moore	ca. 1826	n/a	Burr	n/a	1,000ft	n/a
36-135	Maple Grove / Abbyville Mill	n/a	n/a	n/a	n/a	n/a	n/a	n/a
36-17	John Stoneroad's Mill	Elias McMellen	1868	$1,700	Kingpost	1	65ft	55ft
36-90	Willow Grove / Brenner's	n/a	1847	n/a	Kingpost	1	65ft	55ft
36-91	John Lintner's Mill	James C. Carpenter	1846	$797	Burr	1	86ft	76ft
36-92	John Martin's / Owl Br	n/a	ca. 1846	n/a	Kingpost	1	55ft	48ft
36-93	Stehman's/Conestoga Feed	John Witmer	1852	$1,249	Burr	1	107ft	95ft

Conewago Creek (L) = Lancaster County; (D) = Dauphin County

World Bridge #	Name(s) of Bridge	Builder(s)	Year Built or Rebuilt	Cost	Truss Type	Spans	Overall Length	Abutment to Abutment
36-P2 (L)	Bellaire Bridge	George Hynika	1884	$570	Boxed Pony	1	40ft	35ft
22-P1 (D)								
36-94 (L)	Aberdeen Mill	Elias McMellen	1892	$1,025	Queen Post	1	59ft	52ft
22- ? (D)								
	Conewago Station Railroad	n/a	n/a	n/a	n/a	n/a	n/a	n/a
36-42 (L)	Jacob Nissley's Mill	Messner / Linker	1852	$1,249	Burr	1	94ft	82ft
22-12 (D)								
36-95 (L)	Falmouth Station Bridge	Elias McMellen	1874	$1,490	Burr		108ft	96ft
22- ? (D)								

Donegal Creek

World Bridge #	Name(s) of Bridge	Builder(s)	Year Built or Rebuilt	Cost	Truss Type	Spans	Overall Length	Abutment to Abutment
	Jason McCormick's Mill	n/a	n/a	n/a	n/a	n/a	n/a	n/a
	Chickies Roller Mill	n/a	n/a	n/a	n/a	n/a	n/a	n/a

Roadway Width	Opening Height	Height from Water	Road Information	Comments	Extant
13ft 6in	12ft 10in	17ft	28th Division Hwy / SR 0322	Year gone: 1896	
12ft 8in	12ft 1in	12ft	Cider Mill Rd / LR 36122, SR 1013	Still in use; aka Nathan Eberly's Cider Mill, Fiantz's Mill	✓
13ft	13ft	14ft	W. Farmersville Rd / LR 36032, SR 1013	Flooded (?): 1917	
14ft	13ft	14ft 6in	Glenbrook Rd / SR 0772	Flooded (?): 1917	
13ft 8in	13ft	17ft 6in	Bushong & Quarry Rds / LR 36009, SR 1003	Year gone: 1952	
12ft 5in	12ft 1in	17ft	Bridge Rd / T 620	Still in use; rebuilt by Amish workers in 1973	✓
14ft	13ft	13ft	Hunsecker Rd / LR 36011, SR 1029	Flooded: 6/22/1972; rebuilt in 1973/$321,302; still in use	✓
16ft	12ft 6in	25ft	Old section of New Holland Pike / now T 555	Burned: 11/25/1882	
14ft	13ft	14ft	Eden Rd / T 555	Year gone: 1962	
23ft	n/a	60ft	On what is now Amtrak's main line	Burned: 1854	
15ft	n/a	15ft	Off S. Conestoga Dr - road no longer exists	Flooded: 7/25/1902	
16ft	12ft 4in	22ft 6in	Old Factory Rd - now extension of S. Duke St	Rebuilt by E. McMellen in 1867 for $4,588; year gone: 1948	
13ft 6in	12ft	12ft	E. Strawberry St	n/a	
22ft 8in	12ft 6in	11ft 4in	Willow Street Pike / SR 0222	One of the few two lane bridges; year gone: 1901	
13ft	20ft	21ft	Quarryville Branch of Conrail	Year gone: 1923	
14ft	12ft 6in	15ft	Old section of Hwy 324 / SR 0324	Burned: 1928	
14ft	12ft 5in	13ft	Second Lock Rd / T504	Rebuilt twice by Ben Snavely (1850, 57); Burned: 1/20/1968	
14ft	13ft 5in	17ft	Rice Rd & Short Ln / T504	Rebuilt by J. Huber in 1841 / $2,482; collapsed 1962 & 1969	
14ft	12ft 10in	18ft	S Duke St / Stehman Rd / LR 36008, SR 3032	Year gone: Oct., 1958	
16ft	13ft	19ft	Creek Rd / T561	Year gone: 1922	
14ft	12ft 7in	15ft	River Rd / LR 36005, SR 3017	Rebuilt by James C. Carpenter in 1866 / $6,262; rebuilt by E. McMellen in 1870 for $5,265; flooded: 3/8/1904	
14ft	12ft 3in	7ft	Shreiner Station Rd / T 560	Still in use	✓
n/a	n/a	40ft	1 mile east of Rohrerstown on Conrail branch	Year gone: before 1875	
n/a	n/a	n/a	Columbia Ave / SR 0462	n/a	
12ft	12ft	9ft	Old section of Schoolhouse Rd / T 595	Flooded: 6/22/72	
14ft	12ft	8ft	Millersville Rd / LR 36006, SR 0741	Flooded (?): 1917	
14ft	12ft 6in	10ft	Millersville-Letort Rd / LR 36008, SR 3032	Year gone: 1953	
14ft	11ft 6in	10ft	Owl Bridge Rd / T 583	Flooded (?): 1917	
14ft	12ft 6in	11ft	Walnut Hill Rd / LR 36038, SR 3027	Flooded: 6/26/1938	
14ft	n/a	7ft	Prospect Rd / T 324 (L)	Year gone: 1945 (possibly earlier)	
14ft 2in	12ft	6ft 9in	Mill Rd / T 312 (L), T 564 (D)	Year gone: 1937	
n/a	n/a	n/a	Conrail main line near Conewago	n/a	
15ft	12ft 10in	10ft	Covered Bridge Rd/T300(L), Eagle Rd/T301(D)	Burned: 8/21/1978	
16ft 6in	12ft	14ft	Upstream side of present Hwy 441, SR 0441	Flooded: 3/8/1904	
n/a	n/a	n/a	Marietta Pike / SR 0023	n/a	
n/a	n/a	n/a	Long Lane	n/a	

World Bridge #	Name(s) of Bridge	Builder(s)	Year Built or Rebuilt	Cost	Truss Type	Spans	Overall Length	Abutment to Abutment
Hammer Creek								
	Hopewell Forge	n/a	n/a	n/a	n/a	n/a	n/a	n/a
36-34	Samuel Erb's Mill	John G. Bowman	1887	$1,744	Burr	1	80ft 2in	70ft
Middle Creek								
	Abram Hess'/Eichelberger's	Theodore D. Cochran	ca.1825	$799	Burr	1	58ft 6in	47ft
Mill Creek								
36-96	Henry Eby's / Spence's Mill	B. Graeff / M.P. Cooper	1838	$1,400	Burr	1	112ft	104ft
36-137	Greenlan /Yeates Boys Sch	n/a	n/a	n/a	Burr	n/a	n/a	n/a
36-97	Daniel Pott's Mill / Fertility	J. Elliot / R. Russell	1844	$594	Burr	1	58f	48ft
36-98	Peter Yordy's Mill/Lampeter	James C. Carpenter	1852	$1,045	Burr	1	91ft	77ft
36-99	Henry K. Stoner's Sawmill	J. Elliot / ? Chandler	1843	$849	Burr	1	71ft	58ft
36-100	John W. Eshleman's Mill	Elias McMellen	1866	$1,170	Burr	1	144ft	133ft
36-03	Isaac Baer's / Kurtz's Mill	W.W. Upp	1876	$1,407	Burr	1	96ft 6in	90ft
36-101	Abraham Herr's/Pugh's Mill	Abraham Herr	1838	$1,350	Burr	1	139ft 6in	125ft
36-102	George Herr's Sawmill	Charles Malhorn	1846	$863	Burr	1	104ft	88ft
36-43	Willow Hill / Amish Farm	Roy Zimmerman	1962	n/a	Burr	1	72ft 6in	64ft
Muddy Creek								
36-103	L.G.Good's Grist & Sawmill	John Shaeffer	1851	$1,075	Burr	1	82ft	70ft
36-10	Oberholtzer's Mill /Red Run	Elias McMellen	1866	n/a	Burr	1	119ft	107ft
36-11	John Fry's Mill	J. Fry, M. Fry, & Z. Killian	1849	$934	Burr	1	95ft	81ft
36-104	Gable's Fording	Elias McMellen	1872	$2,995	Burr	1	129ft	117ft
Octoraro Creek East (L) = Lancaster County; (C) = Chester County								
36-38 (L)	John Mercer's Mill	B.C. Carter	1880	$1,652	Burr	1	103ft	86ft 2in
15-19 (C)								
36-105 (L)	Steelville	Geo. Fink / Geo. Hinkle	1847	$800	Burr	1	84ft	70ft
15-78 (C)								
36-39 (L)	Lewis Newcomer's/Bower's	M. Wood / Geo. Jones	1888	$2,835	Burr	1	98ft	90ft
15-20 (C)								
36-40 (L)	Bellbank / Bell's Run Mill	Robert Russell	1850	n/a	Double Burr	1	131ft	112f
15-21 (C)								
36-106 (L)	Albert B. Worth's Mill	E. & S. Mills	1841	$1,100	Double Burr	1	64ft	52ft
15-79 (C)								
36-107 (L)	MtVernon/Bunting's Fording	Jacob Kauffman	1865	$2,650	Burr	1	109ft	93ft
15-80 (C)								
36-41 (L)	Pine Grove	J. Elliot / R. Russell	1846	$1,494	Burr	1	175ft	n/a
15-22 (C)								
	Pine Grove (rebuilt)	Elias McMellen	1884	$4,295	Burr	2	199ft 8in	187ft 4in
36-108 (L)	Jacob L. Kirk's Mill	Jacob L. Kirk	1827	$5,600	Double Burr	1	170ft	56ft
15-81 (C)								
36-109 (L)	Amos Carter's Fording	Jacob L. Kirk / S. Stauffer	1848	$1,793	Double Burr	1	146ft	130ft
15-82 (C)								
36-110 (L)	Wood's Mill	Jacob Kauffman	1890	$3,397	Double Burr	1	149ft	137ft
15-83 (C)								

Roadway Width	Opening Height	Height from Water	Road Information	Comments	Extant
n/a	n/a	n/a	Pumping Station Rd	n/a	
13ft 10in	12ft	7ft 10in	Erb's Bridge Rd / T 634	Still in use	✓
2ft 4in	13ft 2in	10ft	Old section of Meadow Valley Rd / now T 659	Moved in 1966 to Buck Hill Farm 3/4mi S. of Kissel Hill	✓
13ft 9in	13ft	8ft	Old Philadelphia Pike / SR 0340	Year gone: 1922	
n/a	n/a	n/a	Hwy 30 / SR 0030	Year gone: before 1909	
14ft	13ft	9ft 6in	Old Strasburg Pike / LR 36024, SR 2029	Year gone: 1925	
14ft 6in	13ft	8ft 8in	Lampeter Rd / LR 36027, SR 3028	Year gone: 1922	
14ft	13ft	8ft	Gypsy Hill Rd / LR 36034, SR 3039	Year gone: 1920	
14ft 6in	12ft 3in	10ft 6in	Eshleman Mill Rd / T 476	Flooded (?): 1933	
12ft 6in	12ft 5in	17ft	Kiwanis Rd in Lancaster County Central Park	Flooded: 6/22/72; rebuilt by David Esh in 1975/$75,000, still in use	✓
24ft	13ft	14ft 6in	Hollinger Rd / T509; part of old Willow St Pike	Year gone: 1917	
14ft	13ft	10ft	Eckman Rd / T 508	Year gone: 1935	
13ft 6in	12ft 5in	6ft 6in	1/4 mile west of Hwy 896 on Hwy 30	Built out of matrials from Good's Mill & Miller's Farm bridges	✓
14ft	12ft	11ft 6in	Dry Tavern Rd / LR 36012, SR 0897	Year gone: 1952	
12ft	12ft 4in	6ft	Beside Red Run Rd/LR 36013, SR 1044	Still in existence, but on private property	✓
14ft	12ft 6in	12ft 6in	Frysville Rd / T 813	Burned: 3/1/1980	
14ft	12ft 8in	17ft 8in	Martindale Rd / LR 36052, SR 1010	Year gone: 1952	
15ft 6in	12ft 6in	11ft	Bailey's Crossroads / T 976 (L), T 332 (C)	Still in use; shared with Chester County	✓
14ft	13ft	11ft	Steelville Rd / LR 36098, SR 2017 (L)	Year gone: 1941	
16ft	13ft	12ft	Newcomer's Rd / T 772 (L), T 318 (C)	Burned: 11/5/1962	
14ft	12ft	10ft 6in	Street Rd / LR36022, SR 2008 (L)	Rebuilt by R. Russell in 1861/$1,739; burned: 3/20/1970	
12ft 4in	12ft	11ft	Worth's Bridge Rd / T 764 (L), T 310 (C)	Rebuilt in 1857 for $6,500; burned: Sep., 1950	
15ft	13ft	9ft 6in	Kirkwood Pk / Lancaster Pk (SR 0472)	Year gone: 1949; site now under water-Octoraro Reservoir	
15ft	14ft	16ft	Ashville Rd / LR 36018, SR 2006 (L)	Built earlier in 1816-no other information available	
13ft 6in	13ft 3in	16ft 6in		Still in use	✓
14ft 3in	11ft 6in	19ft	Nottingham Rd / SR 0272	Rebuilt by Milton Walker in 1884 for $3,375; year gone: 1932	
14ft	13ft 6in	14ft	Sleepy Hollow Rd / LR 36021, SR 2001	Rebuilt by Milton Walker in 1884 for $975; year gone: 1945	
16ft	12ft 6in	11ft	Gray Horse Rd / T 319 (L), T 300 (C)	Flooded: 1937	

World Bridge #	Name(s) of Bridge	Builder(s)	Year Built or Rebuilt	Cost	Truss Type	Spans	Overall Length	Abutment to Abutment
Octoraro Creek West								
36-33	David W Jackson's Sawmill	Samuel Stauffer	1878	$2,460	Burr	1	160ft 4in	148ft 5in
	Jackson's Sawmill (rebuilt)	Lancaster County	1985	$75,000	Burr	1	142ft 7in	137ft 2in
36-111	Clonmell	Joseph Russell	1853	$640	Kingpost	1	60ft	50ft
36-112	Black Rock Forge	James C. Carpenter	1884	$1,845	Burr	1	70ft	63ft 4in
36-113	Thomas K. Pusey's Mill	Jonathan Webb	1824	$650	Burr	1	65ft	53ft
36-19	Vincent King's	Robert Russell	1848	$885	Burr	1	80ft	68ft
36-18	White Rock Forge	John Russell	1847	n/a	Burr	1	113ft	102ft 8in
36-114	Spruce Grove	Joseph Russell	1847	n/a	Burr	1	61ft	47ft
Pequea Creek								
36-115	New Milltown	James C. Carpenter	1856	$780	Kingpost	1	66ft	55ft
36-20	Eshleman's Mill	James C. Carpenter	1845	$983	Burr	1	113ft 6in	103ft 4in
36-116	London Vale/Leaman Place	Elias McMellen	1866	$1,800	Burr	1	79ft	68ft
36-21	Benjamin Herr's/Souderburg	J. Elliot / R. Russell	1844	$1,787	Double Burr	2	178ft	165ft 6in
36-117	Hartman's	White / Bowers / Vaughn	1841	$1,350	Double Burr	1	140ft	130ft
36-118	Edisonville/Turniptown Mill	Charles Malhorn	1847	$1,000	Burr	1	135ft	123ft
36-22	Bowman's/Henry Neff's Mill	Christian Brackbill	1824	n/a	Burr	1	103ft	91ft
36-119	Lime Valley Mill	Twin #1 Silas Wolverton	1857	n/a	Burr	1	100ft	91ft
36-23	Lime Valley Mill	Twin #2 Elias McMellen	1871	$,2597	Burr	1	103ft 4in	91ft
36-120	Beaver Valley	William English	1827	$1,800	Double Burr	1	98ft	88ft
36-121	Pequea Valley Tavern	Elias McMellen	1868	$2,750	Burr	1	84ft	74ft
36-24	Daniel Good's Fording	Levi Fink	1855	$1,189	Burr	1	79ft	60ft
36-25	Thomas Baumgardner's Mill	Davis Kitch	1860	$1,284	Burr	1	109ft 4in	93ft 8in
36-25	Baumgardner's (rebuilt) Lancaster County		1987	$200,000	Burr	1	116ft 7in	103ft 6in
36-122	John G. Goods Distillery	John Strohm	1840	$1,970	Burr	1	141ft	130ft
36-123	Sickman's Mill	Levi Fink / Henry Hess	1859	$1,189	Burr	1	110ft 6in	90ft
36-124	Gentleman John J. Good's	Elias McMellen	1892	$2,322	Burr	1	102ft	85ft
36-125	Martic Forge	Samuel M. Steele	1844	$1,749	Double Burr	1	163ft	153ft
36-26	Colemanville	James C. Carpenter	1856	$2,244	Double Burr	1	167ft	153ft
36-55	Colemanville (rebuilt)	Lancaster County	1992	$350,000	Burr	1	160ft	142ft
36-126	Samuel Harnish's Sawmill	Elias McMellen	1871	$3,375	Burr	1	112f	100ft
Peters Creek								
36-127	S.W. Boyd's Sawmill	John Weimer	1880	$927	Kingpost	1	51ft	42ft
Susquehanna River (L) Lancaster County; (Y) York County								
36-128 (L) 67-44 (Y)	Columbia / Wrightsville #1	Jonathan Walcott	1813	$231,771	Burr	28	5,690ft	5,678ft
36-129 (L) 67-45 (Y)	Columbia / Wrightsville #2	James Moore	1834	$128,726	Burr	26	5,620ft	5,612ft
36-129 #2 67-45 #2	Columbia / Wrightsville #3	Pennsylvania Railroad	1869	$400,000	Howe	26	5,390ft	5,384ft
36-130	York Furnace - E. Tandem	John Black / Jacob Huber	1855	n/a	Burr/open	14	1,465ft	n/a
36-131 (L) 67-46 (Y)	York Furnace -W. Tandem	John Black / Jacob Huber	1855	n/a	Burr/open	7	600ft	n/a
36-132 (L)	McCalls Ferry Bridge	Theodore Burr	1815	n/a	Double Burr	2	570ft	n/a